looking glass

a positive communication

work-book

Lynda Regan, Sally Jones and Carole Pelling

NSPCC
Cruelty to children must stop. FULL STOP.

City of Salford
Community & Social Services

Barnardo's
GIVING CHILDREN BACK THEIR FUTURE

RHP Russell House Publishing

198 128

First published in 2002 by:

Russell House Publishing Ltd.

4 St. George's House

Uplyme Road

Lyme Regis

Dorset DT7 3LS

Tel: 01297-443948

Fax: 01297-442722

e-mail: help@russellhouse.co.uk

www.russellhouse.co.uk

British Library Cataloguing-in-publication Data:

A catalogue record for this book is available from the British Library.

ISBN: 1-903855-17-9

Typeset by Jeremy Spencer, London

Printed by Ashford Press, Southampton

About Russell House Publishing

RHP is a group of social work, probation, education and youth and community work practitioners and academics working in collaboration with a professional publishing team.

Our aim is to work closely with the field to produce innovative and valuable materials to help managers, trainers, practitioners and students.

We are keen to receive feedback on publications and new ideas for future projects.

For details of our other publications please visit our website or ask us for a catalogue. Contact details are on this page.

Contents

Acknowledgments

The Looking Glass Team would like to thank their respective managers in Social Services, Barnado's and the NSPCC for support and encouragement in undertaking the Looking Glass Project, and in compiling this work-book.

We are grateful to the group of young women we worked with whose resilience, courage, enthusiasm and ideas were an inspiration to us.

We are also extremely grateful to Judith Unsworth Social Services, and Carole Byrne NSPCC for their creativity in producing some lovely visual graphics to accompany the exercises, and for all the extra support in helping us to become more computer literate along the way (not an easy task)!

Thanks as well to all the people whose ideas have contributed to those used in this book, and to the work we undertake with all young people.

Introduction

This book contains ideas and guidance on building positive relationships with young people. It can be used, in a wide variety of settings, by anyone doing direct work with young women.

It will enhance the ability of the young person to deal with one-to-one relationships and provide opportunities for them to:

- feel listened to
- have their views recognised and valued
- explore the dynamics of relationships

The exercises will encourage the young person to express their views, build confidence and begin to make informed choices.

The process is achieved by the worker and the young person, having a period of time to focus on **her**:

- views
- feelings
- emotions
- friendships
- individual situation
- past
- present
- future

...or any other issues that she may choose to share.

It can offer a starting point; or a specific focus of work; or indeed a complete piece of work. The ideas it contains have been used in positive work with young women, but are not put forward as solutions for specific issues or behaviours.

Although the Looking Glass Work-book was developed through work with young women in residential care, and evaluated by them, the exercises can be used with young women in a range of other settings; and indeed, many are transferable to work with boys and young men.

The book is primarily intended for use with 12 to 16 year-old girls. Some of the initial sessions can be used with younger girls, but you may find that those about friendships and relationships are a little too complex for them.

The work-book contains eight session plans. These include an opening session where boundaries for the work are set, and agreement reached on issues such as:

- recording
- confidentiality
- content

...and a closing session where work can be reviewed, sessions formally ended or further sessions planned and agreed.

The remaining sessions focus on:

- Exploring with the young person their wishes, expectations and feelings, about themselves, their lives and their relationships.
- Identifying their strengths and positive attributes.
- Being a forum for discussing relationships, both positive and negative.
- Exploring choices and dilemmas.
- Keeping safe and making informed choices.

The ideas used here are by no means exhaustive. In the area of direct work it is important to use your own creative skills and adapt ideas from a range of sources. **Be creative and enjoy!**

Positive communication

looking glass framework

Positive Communication with Young People

How can we set up a positive environment and use our skills to work most effectively with young people?

Why are you there?

Some aims may be:

- Offering the young person support.
- Providing a basis for growth, self-help, independence and self-protection.
- Allowing expression of feelings in a safe environment.
- Communicating positive messages to the young person.
- Enabling the young person to adopt new roles.
- Teaching the young person that they have a right not to be abused in the future.
- What are other people saying about the young person's needs?
- What are you being asked to do?

Where is the young person at?

- Physically, emotionally, intellectually.
- What is the young person saying about her experiences?
- Is the young person ready for 'help'?
- What does the young person know/not know about their abuse and current situation? What are the gaps in their knowledge?
- What are the particular needs of this young person that you may need to consider in planning this work?

What is the best way to ensure positive communication?
When building up a relationship with a young person it is *important* that the young person feels:

- Safe and secure.
- That you are trustworthy.

- Listened to.
- You are not judgemental.
- You are a safe ally.
- You are reliable.
- Accepted for who they are.
- They can have fun.
- They know the boundaries.

When communicating with young people it is important to remember:

- You are on the same level or lower.
- You do not invade their space.
- You give them your full attention and *listen*.
- You are relaxed and calm.
- You do not interrupt.
- You use only safe touching.
- You use a pleasant, gentle manner.
- You are non-confrontational.
- You do not control and direct.
- You join in and have fun too.

Session 1
Introductory Session

- Agreement

- Setting the scene

- Boundaries, and aims of the work

- Recording, confidentiality

looking glass framework

Agreements

A work agreement is an essential start to any piece of direct work with a young person. It is important that the young woman you are working with has a clear understanding of the boundaries around the individual work. For example, how often and how long the sessions will be, what is considered appropriate behaviour, confidentiality, supervision and recording arrangements.

The young woman needs to be part of the agreement process, so that she feels she has some say and control in the way the sessions are to be conducted. She needs to have an understanding of why the individual work has been suggested, the contents of the work, what commitment it entails and how the sessions might meet her needs.

Working together on the agreement is the start of the positive communication process, where the young woman begins to feel listened to and valued.

What we Agree to Talk About

This is an agreement between _____

_____

Dates of sessions _____ Time _____

_____ _____

_____ _____

_____ _____

_____ _____

If unable to attend: _____

_____

Information

> What will be written down, where will this be kept, who will do the writing, who will be able to see this, what happens to the work produced.

Confidentiality

> What things can we talk about and what things would the worker need to talk to someone else about. What will happen if the worker needs to talk to someone about something from the sessions, what happens if the worker thinks there may be a issue about your safety. Will the worker be talking to their line manager about the work.

Complaints

> What happens if the young woman wishes to stop the sessions, if she wants to make a complaint, or check something out with someone else about the work or the worker. Who does she contact and how? What happens if the worker feels they need to stop the sessions, how does the young woman get to know.

Agreement for Sessions

Dealing with
feelings

Relationships

Making choices

What do I think?

Friendships

**What our
sessions will
be about**

Having fun

Living in care

Taking care of ME

Expectations

How do others
see ME?

Signed _____

Signed _____

Date _____

What we Agree to Talk About

This is an agreement between _____

_____

Dates of sessions _____   Time _____

_____   _____

_____   _____

_____   _____

_____   _____

If unable to attend: _____

_____

Information

```



```

Confidentiality

```




```

Complaints

```



```

Agreement for Sessions

Signed _____

Signed _____

Date _____

Techniques to use during ANY of the sessions for fun, or if stress levels are high and you want an outlet for this.

Cornflour Mixture

Half a packet of cornflour, water, food colouring.

Place cornflour in a bowl, add water slowly until the mixture is smooth and thick. Add food colouring. Play!

This has a lovely gloopy texture which is very soothing and fun to feel.

Play-dough Recipe

3 cups of plain flour	1 cup of salt
Food colouring	1 tablespoon of cooking oil
1 teaspoon of cream of tartar	half-pint of water

1. Place the flour, salt and cream of tartar in a large pan.
2. Place pan on a low heat and pour the water in slowly, mixing everything together until it forms a doughy consistency.
3. Add cooking oil and food colouring.
4. Take off the heat and knead dough together.

Note: Store in a plastic bag or container in the fridge. Keeps for approx. three months.

Clay

Can be used to model 'feelings' or people. The young woman can decide when she has finished modelling, what she wants to do with it – keep it, squash it, re-make it until she feels calmer.

Painting

Can be used to express angry feelings – but you will need large sheets of paper and plenty of space. The young woman may want to paint using brushes or using her hands. As before, she can choose at the end what she wants to do with the finished painting. She may want to keep it, throw it away, rip it up, allow her to choose.

✳

Session 2
Getting to Know You

- How does the young woman see herself?

- How does she think others see her?

looking glass framework

Word Sheets/Images Exercise

Theme: Getting to Know You

Aim
To encourage the young woman to have a better understanding of herself, focusing more on the positives rather than the negatives.

Materials
Word sheets, feelings, images, word cards and pens.

Method
Using the word sheets/images, encourage the young woman to identify the words that she believes describe herself, her personality. Do not disagree with what she says. If she struggles to find any positive words, ask her to think about what her best friend might say about her. Point out words that you think describe her. After the exercise, discuss the outcome, focusing on her strengths.

Adapted by SJ/CP/LR from ideas used in positive communication techniques

Feeling good   Given up   Can ask for help

            Ugly   Moody

Good sense of humour   No-one cares

                            Invisible

                        Understanding   Amazing

                                                        Angry

Good listener

        Feel different   Don't like myself

    Aggressive   No-one likes me   Swearing

            Funny   Fun

Can't be bothered   Good mate   Supportive

            Not liked   Can't show feelings

    Feels healthy   Gets on with people   Unhappy

            Rude   Belongs

                            Dangerous

Thoughtful

Sad

Can look after myself

Feeling bad

Ungrateful

Cheerful

Cool

Likeable

Unattractive

Don't fit in

Bright

Helpful

Not listened to

Stresshead

Friendly

Co-operative

Kind

Not listening

Looking bad

Giving

Clever

Happy

Stressed

Unloved

Unhelpful

Bored

Looking good

Unwanted

Trustworthy

Word Sheet Exercise

Theme: Getting to Know You

Aim
See Word Sheets/Images Exercise.

Materials
Large sheet of paper and word cards already made up. You may want to include some blank ones to fill in as you go along.

Method
This exercise works in the same way as the Word Sheets/Images Exercise. There should be a mixture of positive and negative words. Encourage the young woman to pick out the words that she identifies with, disregarding others. When she has finished, encourage her to sort out her word file into words that she owns and accepts, and others that she feels have been given to her by others, or forced upon her. It is important to focus on her strengths and acknowledge these to her.

Below is a suggested format for the exercise, you may wish to use other headings.

Lot like me	Like me sometimes	Not like me at all	Not sure
friendly calm	helpful bored	afraid	

afraid	scared	excited	bored	puzzled
thoughtful	sad	friendly	helpful	calm
cheerful	angry	bright	cool	crazy

Developed by LR and young person

The Rosebush

Theme: Getting to Know You

Aim
To help someone use their imagination in a way that may reflect some part of their experience. We have included some of the examples given in Oaklander's book to help clarify how this can work.

Materials
Paper and felt tip pens, paints, or collage materials.

Method
This exercise can be done in a number of different ways dependant on the young woman's own preferences and materials available. It can be an exercise where she draws, colours, paints, makes a collage of what she visualises. Or it can be something she chooses just to describe.

Explain that this is an exercise where we use our imagination. It is meant to be fun and relaxing, not a test of any kind. If the young person is comfortable with this and willing to give it a try, ask her to close her eyes and imagine she is going into a space that is all her own. Tell her to concentrate on being in her own space, imagine it is like a white canvas, big, empty, no-one has ever seen it before.

Ask her to imagine she is a rosebush in that place.

Using prompts, as appropriate, ask her to describe what kind of rosebush she is, and what she looks like.

Some prompts may be:
- Are you small/large?
- Is your stem thick/thin?
- Are you a new rosebush, or are you fully developed?
- Do you have any flowers, what colour are they, are there lots or just a few?
- Are you strong and healthy?
- Do you have any leaves or thorns?
- Where are you – in a garden, in the country, in a field, in a vase?
- Is there anything around you – other rosebushes or plants, a fence, trees?
- What is the weather like?
- Who takes care of you?

When she has a full picture, if she wishes you can ask her to draw, paint or make a collage of it.

Young people may choose to give some clues about how they see themselves using this medium. If they feel un-cared for, alone or unprotected, this is a less threatening way of communicating that than saying it directly.

If the picture given appears to touch on some sadness or loss for the young person you can help her with this by asking after the exercise has been completed, what would make the rosebush feel better/ more cared for/less lonely, and that might be the picture she wants to imagine and draw.

Ten-year-old Cheryl has lived in several foster homes since her mother abandoned her when she was about 5. Because of legalities she was unable to be permanently adopted until recently. She is a very bright, attractive youngster who has been in therapy because of sleepwalking and severe nightmares. She said of her rosebush, "I am very big. I have all sorts of different colour flowers. I don't have straight branches; they're slanted, curvy. I'm in soft dirt and I have long roots buried in the ground very deeply. I have lots of friends – birds sit on the fence and talk to me. There's a big black fence around me so people won't step on me or pick me. I live in a yard. I'm just an ordinary rosebush. I have green leaves." I asked who takes care of you? "Nature takes care of me – the rain and sun and soil." (I asked) who lives in the house? "Some people." (I asked) do you like them? "I never meet them; they're always going some place. I'm by myself".

Out of this experience, we were able to deal openly with some issues that were held very deeply within Cheryl. One was her "big black fence." Which protected her. She talked about her need for protection so she would not be hurt. Although it had been obvious these things had been bothering her, Cheryl would not talk about them until now. (V. Oaklander, *Windows to our Children*, p36-7)

By suggesting this exercise we do not mean to assume that everyone can, or should try to become a therapist.

The above example shows how links may be made and clues given as to how the young person sees her situation.

This exercise provides ways to acknowledge the content of what the young woman offers without making rash judgements. If you think she is making links with her own experience you can always ask, for example it is okay to say something like —your rosebush seems to be lonely/surrounded by nice things etc. is that how things feel for you sometimes? **If she is ready to acknowledge the links she will tell you if you are right, if she isn't ready then no harm has been done, you have simply shown her you are interested in her.**

The suggestions offered also give a way to then use positive thinking as a coping strategy.

Don't feel you have to offer solutions to all her difficulties. When we feel down ourselves we often just want someone to listen, be there and care – not offering to solve things for us.

V. Oaklander (1988)

Skills worksheet

Theme: Getting to Know You

Aim:
To help the young woman recognise some of her positive attributes and strengths.

I am good at:

_____
_____
_____
_____
_____

I enjoy:

_____
_____
_____
_____
_____

I wish I could:

_____
_____
_____
_____

Things I do well:

_____
_____
_____
_____

Things I do for others:

_____
_____
_____
_____
_____

Adapted by SJ/CP/LR from ideas used in positive communication techniques

A Poster

Theme: Getting to Know You

Aim:
- For the young woman to be aware of her self image.
- Have the opportunity to explore their thoughts and views about themselves.
- It helps the worker look at the child's self vision – the young woman's view may be self-critical.
- It may present an opportunity for the worker to praise the young woman or discuss their strengths and build self-esteem.

  (Please try and keep in mind from small acorns large oak trees grow.)

Materials
Art paper or A3 paper, crayons, felt tips, pencil, scissors, magazines, old clothes, catalogues, comics etc., paint, glitter etc.

Method
The young woman has a choice of how she wants to make her poster – by painting or collage.

- Collage is often an easier method of representing a self image.
- The worker's role is to encourage the young woman to express her feelings and views about herself. Examples:
  - What sort of clothes do you like?
  - What sort of music do you like?
  - What are you good at (give some examples of her skills and strengths if the young woman is lacking confidence).

Notes:
- It is important that the worker is supportive but you don't want a poster, which illustrates only the workers' views.
- Accept the young woman may have a low level of self-esteem.

Developed from ideas in V Oaklander (1988) and J Carroll (1988)

Session 3
Feelings

- What feelings can we identify?

- What do we do with our feelings?

- How they can affect our relationships?

looking glass framework

Reading our Feelings

Theme: Feelings

Aims

- Reflect on what range of emotions the young person can identify.

- Help her link appropriate responses to situations and reinforce the notion that reactions do not always have to be extreme.

- That reactions to situations are okay if they are controlled.

- Explore the 'clues' given by our expressions and body language, so that our 'early warning signs' can be understood.

Notes:

Faces can express a whole range of emotions. Using the blank pro-formas is a useful way to begin to identify a whole range of emotions. When we identify or express feelings verbally, we often state the most obvious, such as happy, sad, angry, and so on. Some young people don't learn to identify the more subtle emotions, such as tense, a bit down, thoughtful, distracted, confused, etc. They can often see things in very definite terms, things are either brilliant or a disaster, on or off, right or wrong. This means that reactions to events can sometimes be extreme.

The subtler emotions are often accompanied by gestures, body posture and expressions that are the 'early warning signs' of someone else's mood. If these signals are not noticed, ignored or misunderstood, the other person's tensions increase and can result in conflict.

By helping someone identify these subtle 'clues', it may help them avoid conflict.

Materials

Blank pro-formas, pens, pencils.

Ideas developed from exercises in B James (1989) and Feelings Faces Cards – Arnolds

Method

Stage 1: Using a blank pro-forma sheet

The young woman and worker could draw faces showing a range of emotions. Take your lead from the young person. What emotions can she identify, is she aware of a whole range of emotions or just the main ones. You can have loads of fun deciding how to depict people's feelings!

This may be a short exercise in itself leading to discussions about the faces drawn and what the emotions suggest or imply, what she can describe from her own experience, what her reactions were, what someone else's reactions were, and so on.

Using ready drawn images and words:
If the young woman is likely to need prompts you could have a set of faces ready drawn (they really do only need to be basic so don't worry about your artistic abilities), and then use 'post-it notes', or labels for her to match the words with the expressions.

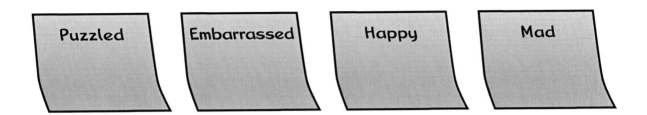

Using images instead of or as well as faces:
The figure sheets provided in Session 1 can be used to talk about what that image suggests to the young woman.

Stage 2 (Progressing the exercise if appropriate)

Aims

- Helping the young woman identify what signals we pick up from other people.
- Identifying appropriate responses to others.
- Recognising when we have choices about avoiding or encouraging conflict.

Identifying signals from others:
You could talk about, draw or paint how we notice someone else's emotions/feelings. How can we tell if someone is:

- in a bad mood
- feeling anxious
- bored
- excited
- fed up
- upset
- down
- getting ready to blow

What are the body and facial signals that give us clues.

Are these signals true for everyone, or what are the generalisations we can learn from them.

How do we respond to these signals?
This could involve helping the young woman consider:

- How she would respond to other people giving out these signals.
- How she would want someone to respond to her if she was feeling...............

Are these responses the same? If not what is different and why.

These issues are likely to produce discussions about situations the young woman is familiar with, possibly within the residential home, it can sometimes be less threatening and less personalised, if scenario's are used that incorporate other names, or maybe, cartoon characters.

This allows the opportunity to opt out of what the young person and worker know as reality, and allows opportunity to consider the situation objectively.

Once this has been done, together you can draw the links with reality, e.g. "okay so in this situation you think ... should do ... It's a bit like when ... happens between you and ... What usually happens then? Given what we have been thinking about how do you think things could be different next time that happens?"

Choices about how we respond:
Using the scenarios as a focus look at choices about responses, and at the different potential outcomes.

Acknowledge that the young woman can only be responsible for *her own* responses and not the other person's.

The main issue is one of choice and control. What outcome does she want in certain situations and how does she try to get that while still being able to feel good about what she has done/said?

What way of responding would make her feel good about herself, and what would make her feel bad?

Developed by L.R.

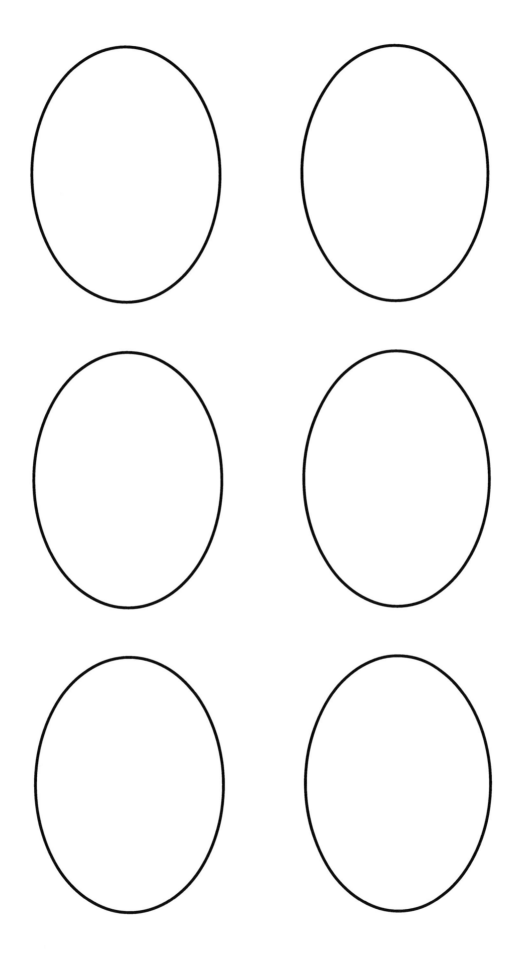

Session 3

Theme: Feelings

Aim
To encourage the young woman to explore her feelings, how she shows them, and how she and others can be affected by them.

Materials
Picture of bottle/can, worry bag and coloured pens.

Method:

1. Feelings – Bottle/Can
Using the picture of the pop bottle, encourage the young woman to think about her feelings that she shows and the ones that she doesn't show, that perhaps she keeps hidden. Ask her to write them inside the bottle/can, perhaps in bubbles. Encourage the young woman to think about what would happen if the bottle of pop was shaken continuously. Eventually the pop would explode out of the bottle, spilling everywhere. This is a simple way of explaining that if you bottle your feelings up inside, eventually you end up losing control, which often has disastrous consequences. Discuss ways of letting out feelings slowly.

Source unknown

2. Feelings – Worry Bag
Sometimes the young woman may feel that she has so many problems there is nothing she can do. By encouraging the young woman to identify her worries/problems and placing them in the bag, it shows how so many worries can bring you down. Encourage the young woman to look at the problems one by one, by prioritising and sharing, some of the worries could be removed.

Notes:
Another visual way to do the Worry Bag exercise is to use a real bag and potatoes with blank stickers on them. Encourage the young woman to write the worries on the potatoes and place them in the bag. Ask her to carry the bag around and see how heavy it feels. Work together to lighten the load.

Adapted by S.J. from V Ironside (1994)

The Star

Theme: Feelings

Aim
The aim of this exercise is to provide an enjoyable way for the young person to recognise their skills and strengths.

Materials
Pre-printed star or paper to make one. Art materials to decorate the star (eg felt tips, glue, glitter, picture for collage).

Method
The young person has a choice to decide which sort of star they wish to use, or design their own. Then the worker encourages the young person to reflect on their skills and strengths – examples: helpful, caring, calm, good at listening, good at going to school, being honest etc. A lot of adults and young people struggle to recognise the positive aspects of themselves and so the worker might give examples of the young person's strengths. Please comment and recognise beginnings of skills and interests for the young person as research demonstrates that we all change our behaviours and maintain these changes through praise and not criticism.

The words or positive statements are then put onto the star in any way the young person wishes to – example: a word on each point. When completed, this exercise provides the young person with a positive finished item to take away from the session which can also serve as an object to re-enforce a stronger, and more positive sense of self.

The star exercise can also be used with young people to recognise and demonstrate their wishes, for example: one big wish on the star or five wishes.

Notes:
The young person may wish to keep the star or may wish for the worker to keep their star which demonstrates a level of trust between worker and the young person. The main purpose of the star is to increase the level of communication between the worker and the child whilst encouraging positive statements from and about the young person.

Adapted from Striker and Kimmel (1978)

Taking Your Temperature

Theme: Feelings

Aims

- To help the young person understand a range of feelings.
- To help associate levels of feelings with the words used.
- To help check out appropriate responses to situations.

Materials

Use the blank pro-forma or draw a large thermometer on a sheet of paper.

Method

Ask the young woman to think of as many different feelings related to getting angry, that she can, i.e. livid, fuming, ready to blow, irritated.

Either write these directly onto *one* side of the thermometer, or onto post-it notes and decide where they fit onto the thermometer scale.

You could try to think of situations that make you feel each of these things and write these on the opposite side of the scale.

Check out what feelings are linked with what events and decide if responses to those situations are appropriate, or are there times when responses are at a different level than they need to be.

MacFarlane and Cunningham (1991)

The stronger the feeling the higher the temperature

Session 3

Theme: Feelings

Aim
To provide opportunity for the young woman to think about her feelings and how she controls them.

Materials
Use the pro-forma.

Method
Let the young woman complete the pro-forma and use the answers as a focus for following through ideas and discussions.

Developed by L.R.

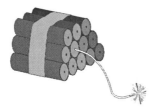

Feelings

If something upsets me I can choose to:

1. get angry and retaliate

2. let someone get to me/pick on me, and do nothing

3. feel angry and take time to think about what I really want to say or do, so that I get my point across clearly

Which do you most often choose?   1   2   3

Which do you think is the best option and why?   1   2   3

Which of the choices above would I do if I was:

1. ignoring my feelings/bottling my feelings up   1   2   3

2. taking control of what I do and say, so that I can feel I have
   stood up for myself in a good way   1   2   3

3. letting my anger take control of me   1   2   3

When I get angry I feel _____

I can tell when I am getting angry by _____

Other people can tell by _____

The thing that works best to calm myself down is _____

_____

What I think I am like with people when I am angry (*i.e. cruel, use bad language, call them names, irrational, out of control etc.)*

_____

One thing I would change if I could about how I react is _____

When I am angry I wish other people would – Listen to me/keep away from me/understand/ let me calm down and then talk to me (put a circle around the ones true for you)

_____

Session 4
Who am I?

- What part of ourselves do we show to others?

- What part of ourselves do we keep private?

- Bringing the two together, and understanding ourselves more

looking glass framework

Session 4

Theme: Who am I?

Aim

To encourage the young woman to explore her feelings, how she shows them and how she and others can be affected by them.

Materials

Square piece of paper and coloured pens.

Method

1. Take one corner of the square piece of paper and fold into the middle, repeat with other three corners.

2. Turn the paper over and fold each corner again into the middle.

3. Fold in half both ways.

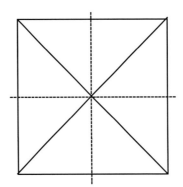

4. Place fingers (thumb and index finger of each hand) inside square flaps and move in and out.

5. On the outside square flaps encourage the young woman to use different colours to represent her moods.

6. On the inside triangles encourage the young woman to write down her feelings e.g. angry, upset, happy etc.

7. Inside the triangles' flaps encourage the young woman to think about and write how she might show her inner feelings, directly or indirectly. Sometimes these inner feelings are not easy or comfortable to name, and the young woman may struggle with the exercise.

Notes:

It is important to note that communication between the worker and the young woman is more important than completing the exercise.

Adapted from traditional source

Life Ladder

Theme: Who am I?

Aim
To build up self-esteem and confidence, encouraging a greater sense of self worth.

Materials
Picture of ladder and coloured pens.

Method
The life ladder symbolises the uphill climb that life can be. It is important that the young woman feels that she deserves a better life/to be happy, and that she is important. Use the life ladder to encourage the young woman to fill in positive 'I' statements, for example:

- I can do
- I deserve
- I am
- I am not responsible for

Encourage the young woman to think about what her long term or short term goal might be, what she would like to achieve for herself (not others). Maybe she would like to put her 'goal' at the top of the ladder, encouraging her that most things are achievable.

Developed from BAAF (1989)

The Shield

Theme: Who Am I?

Aim
To help the young woman recognise her strengths.

Materials
Pro-forma of shield, coloured pens or collage materials/paints.

Method
This is a well known exercise that can be used in many different ways. In this piece of work it can be used to be a visual reminder to the young woman of what strengths she has and what courage she has had to survive events in her past, e.g. sometimes the difficulties we experience make us stronger, (we wouldn't choose to go through hurtful times but also we do not always recognise the strength or skills we have within ourselves to get through these times).

The shield is a visual barrier against the world and a protector from hurt.

Divide the shield into four – give each section a title and allow the young woman to complete it. As she goes along try to help her acknowledge what strengths she has now, and what strengths she has had in the past that have helped her get through difficult times. Reflecting this may help her realise that even though at times things may seem really bad, she can and will get through. That even though she has had difficult times in the past, not all her life has been bad, there will have been some good times along the way as well. Some suggestions are listed below, you may think of others that are more relevant.

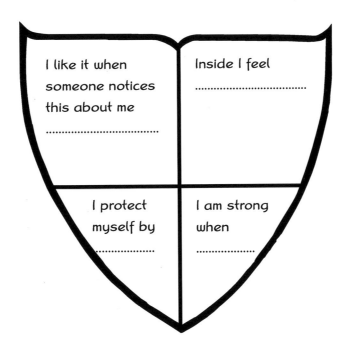

Flower Petals/CD Box

Theme: Who am I?

Aim
To acknowledge the young woman's skills and strengths, and to provide a forum for the worker to reflect on these and (where appropriate) add to these from your own observations/knowledge.

Materials
Flower petal pro-forma each, or circular shapes and an empty CD box.

Method
Using the flower petal pro-forma the young person could complete the sentences, or you could offer suggestions.

Young people like to feel they are noticed as an individual and reflecting on some of the smaller things they do can be very empowering and confidence building, e.g. I told one young woman that I thought she was a very thoughtful person because she always asked others if they wanted a drink when she made one for herself, another young woman was really pleased when I told her she always looked after her hair and it was shiny.

It is important that the statements are personal to the young woman and acknowledge the positive parts of her.

CD Box
Another way of doing this is to cut out some circular card shapes, each of you write positive statements on them. These can be placed in a CD box that the young woman can keep to look at when she is having a bad time.

The box, of course, can be personalised by the young woman which can again be a fun part of the sessions.

I have worked with many young women who have valued my positive statements about them and have kept them long after my involvement ended.

Sometimes we all need reminders of what we have done, achieved, have recognised the nice things we do for others. This is a nice exercise for staff teams to do. Each worker completes a positive statement for the others. At the end of the process each worker has their own box of positive statement from colleagues.

Developed by SJ/CP/LR

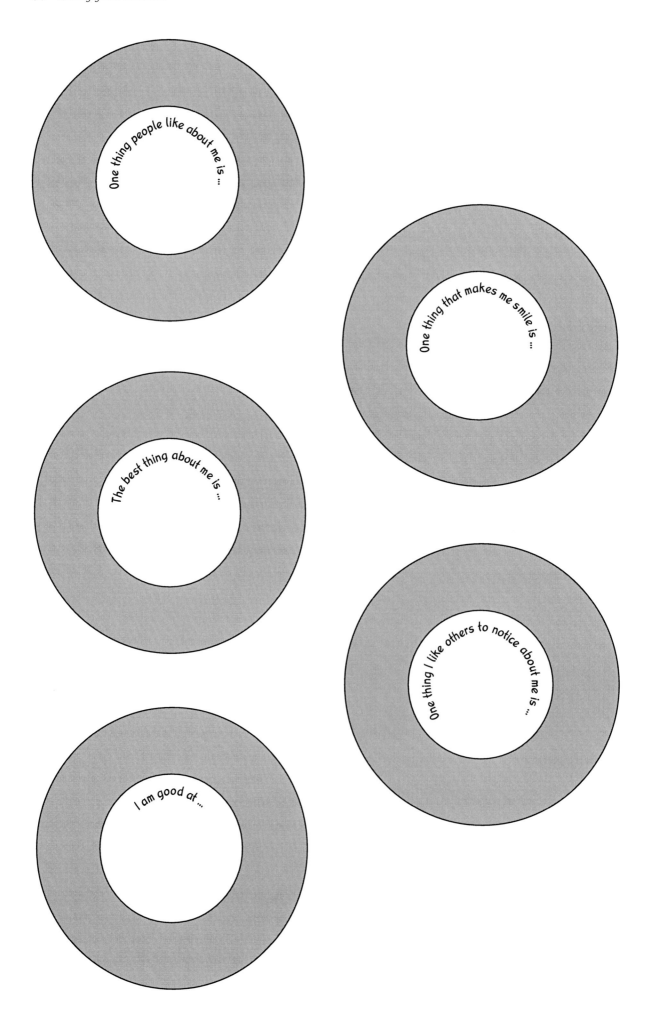

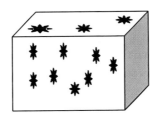

The Box

Theme: Who am I?

Aim
To help children and young people clarify their feelings and to have something to keep for themselves.

Materials
Any small box or shoe box (gift boxes can be cheaply purchased), a range of colouring materials, pens, felt tips, glue and magazines/old catalogues etc.

Method
- The inside of the box represents how you feel or think privately. The outside of the box is how you present yourself to the world or things that people see about you.

- Cut out pictures and paste or write words to put on the outside of the box that describe how you are seen by others or talents that you display or things you don't mind sharing.

- Do the same for the inside, except these will be things that you usually don't share or only share with special people.

Notes:
The box is something that the child or young person can share with a person or just keep (or throw away).

Adapted from B James (1989)

It's my Life Jigsaw

Theme: Who Am I?

Aim
To assist the young woman to express her views about her situation in a focused way.

Materials
Jigsaw pro-forma, pens/pencils.

Method
Encourage the young woman to complete the jigsaw statements acknowledging the parts of her life that are okay and the parts that create difficulties for her.

This exercise was devised with a young person to consider all the statements in relation to her experience.

The exercise was not aimed at judging levels of care or workers, but as a forum for her to consider what she feels to be the positive and negative experiences, and to then consider what she brings to this or how she may be able to influence changes.

The value as so often is the case in direct work, lay in following through the issues that evolved from the piece of work rather than filling in all the boxes.

It allowed the young woman to vent frustrations at the unfairness in her life, but also provided a way of looking at how she coped with these feelings, what she could do to influence some parts of her life, and how she could have her views heard and acknowledged – even though she could not have what she wanted which was to go home and be loved.

Developed by L.R. and young person

It's my Life!

The very best thing in my life is ...

I would like more choice about ...

It would be better if ...

I really don't want ...

I would like this person to listen more to what I say/want/need/feel ...

I am liked by ...

One thing I need help to understand better is ...

Things that are not so good in in my life are ...

I really don't want ...

The person who talks to me about what is happening is ...

Session 5
Friendships and
Relationships

- What do we want?

- How do they develop?

- How do we make positive choices?

looking glass framework

Islands

Theme: Relationships

Aim
The aims of this exercise are to provide a visual image to explore the young person's world and ideas.

This is often a safer way for the young person to work rather than direct questions or interview techniques.

Materials
Pre-painted island picture, felt tips, pens or paper, crayons, and glue to create an island picture.

Method
The young person chooses an island, either one from the pack or they may wish to draw their own. The theme of this exercise is often about relationships. Ideas for generating discussions are:

- who the young person would take to their island
- why?
- what would it be like?
- a description of the island and the sea
- how do you get there?

If the young person wants to be alone on the island the ask:

- why?
- what would they do?
- reflect self-care skills
- how long would they stay?

Notes:
The exercise belongs to the young person to use. It is important for the worker to be neutral not judgemental (examples: Oh you couldn't live there – do that etc.)

If the young person wants to destroy the island it's alright, try and look at why.

This exercise is about 30 minutes where the young person can feel in control of this fantasy life on the island.

Adapted from J Carroll (1988) and BAAF (1989)

Friendship Worksheet

Theme: Relationships

Aim
To think about friends and friendships.

Method
Young woman completes the worksheet thinking about what she wants and her experiences.

What makes me a good friend?

What do I want from a friend?

One nice thing I have done for a friend this week:

One nice thing a friend has done for me:

Something I'd like to improve so I could be a better friend:

How will I do it?

When will I try?

How did it work?

What will I do differently next time?

Developed by L.R.

Relationship Circle

Theme: Friendships and relationships

Aim

- What is a safe/unsafe relationship
- What she wants from a relationship
- How she would like to be treated

Method

Using the sheet with the inner and outer circle, encourage the young woman to think about safe, unsafe relationships. In the outer circle write in what behaviours are not okay (unsafe). In the inner circle write behaviours that feel okay (safe). If the young woman is struggling with this exercise, ask her how she would like to be treated, what she needs from a relationship to feel safe and secure.

Notes:

When the relationship circle is completed ask the young woman to explore the relationships she is currently involved in and where she would place them in the circle.

Adapted by S.J. original source unknown

Relationships

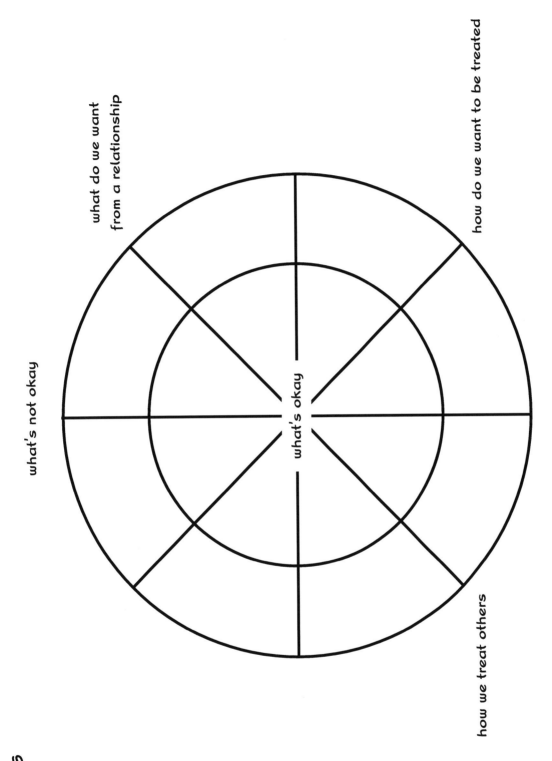

what do we want
from a relationship

how do we want to be treated

what's not okay

what's okay

how we treat others

Relationships

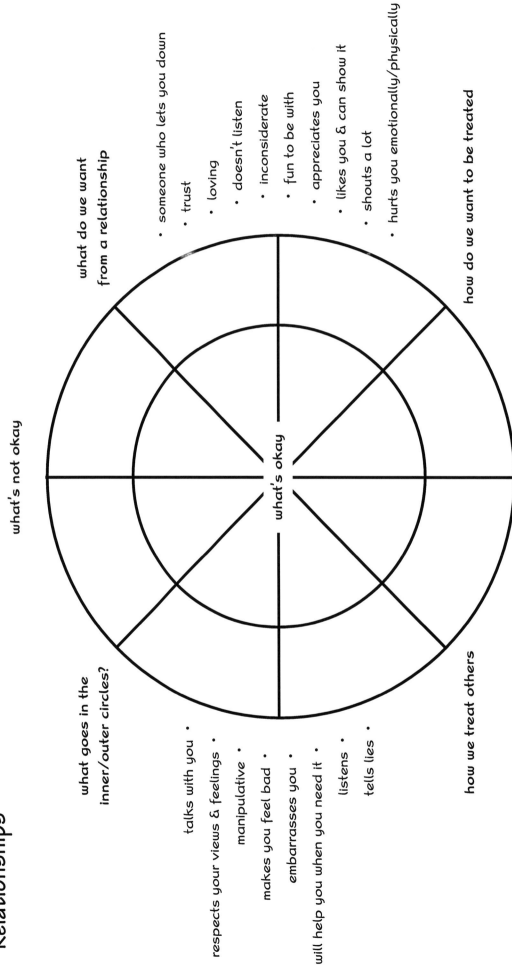

what do we want
from a relationship

- someone who lets you down
- trust
- loving
- doesn't listen
- inconsiderate
- fun to be with
- appreciates you
- likes you & can show it
- shouts a lot
- hurts you emotionally/physically

how do we want to be treated

what's not okay

what's okay

what goes in the
inner/outer circles?

- talks with you
- respects your views & feelings
- manipulative
- makes you feel bad
- embarrasses you
- will help you when you need it
- listens
- tells lies

how we treat others

Session 6
Keeping Relationships

- How our actions impact on our relationships with others

- How we can begin to take control and make choices about this

looking glass framework

Flags Exercise

Theme: Keeping Relationships

Aim

- To help the young woman think about the words she uses.
- To think about the impact of these, whether she is saying clearly what she means.
- To seek ways to modify this, where appropriate.

Materials

Large sheet of paper, some ready prepared statement cards, pens, red/green flags or stickers with red/green Xs on.

Method

Stage 1: Saying What We Mean.

Using the statement cards (some suggestions listed below), look at each one and decide if it is okay to say it as it is. Ask the young woman to give it a green flag/sticker for okay, and a red flag/sticker for not okay.

If the statement gets a red flag/sticker, decide what the person really means to say and think of other, more appropriate ways of communicating this.

(We all feel better about ourselves if we have responded to conflict or confrontation in a positive way, getting our point across clearly. However this is not always easy to do. Sometimes tempers flare and responses are not connected to the original issue. Help the young woman look at how she can keep focus, say what she means in a reasonable, assertive way that helps her to feel good about herself afterwards. The Feelings Worksheet – Session 3 could also be used alongside this exercise)

Examples

Is it OK to say these things? Are they red flag or green flag statements? What do you think the person really means to say? How can this be said more sensitively?

They're a bunch of idiots	You're thick!
She's such a slob	I hate him – he looks like a geek!

What We Say and What We (may) Mean

RED	GREEN
You're such a slob	It annoys me that you are so messy, I wish you would ... look after your clothes better/wear more trendy clothes/wash your hair more often ...
I hate you	I am really angry with you because ... I was really hurt when you ...
I hate him he looks like a geek!	We don't get along/ he's not my type
You are so stupid you really do my head in	I am really angry with you, I wish you would listen to what I say!
Get out and don't ever come back	I'm really annoyed just now and I need some time away from you. We will talk later when we have both had time to think
Stop it! I hate you and never want to see you again	It feels like you do this just to annoy me, it would be better if you ...

Stage 2: Stop. Think. Respond.

Stage 1 of this exercise may identify statements that are problematic for the young woman, either ones that are said to her or ones that she says to others. Or you may want to use ready prepared statements that you know are problematic. Use this to help her identify problems and solutions.

Example:
*   What happens when you say .... to ....
*   How could you say it differently so that .... is clear about what really annoys/ upsets you?
*   What kind of things have you said/done that you feel bad about afterwards?
*   Did you really mean those things or were you just angry?
*   How do you think it made .... feel?
*   What things might have made you feel better?
*   What do you think you could do differently?

If it is appropriate help the young woman identify steps for change and taking control. You could use the 'Plan for Change' pro-forma from Session 6.

Step 1: **STOP** recognise the problem – collect your thoughts, count to 10.
Step 2: **THINK** about what has been said, what is actually meant, what you want to achieve from this.
Step 3: **RESPOND** in a clear, controlled way that allows you to get your point across in a more mature way, and feel good about how you achieve this.

Adapted by S.J. and L.R. from ideas in Chalk Face (1994),
MacFarlane and Cunningham (1991), and Anger Management Techniques

Statements Regarding Relationships

Theme: Keeping Relationships

Aim
A quick way to help the young woman focus on positive and negative aspects of their relationships.

Materials
The list of statements from the pro-forma (you can probably add many more). Two boxes.

Being ignored	Being listened to
Being left out	Being included
Being made fun of	Being appreciated
Being put down	Being told nice things
Being teased	Being respected
Being hit	Being treated kindly
Being bullied	Being able to laugh together
Being made to do things I don't like	Doing nice things
Playing 'mind' games	Being given presents
Being nasty	Treated fairly
Being hurtful	Being cared for
Treated badly	Being loved
Made to feel stupid	Being liked
Made to feel I don't belong	Being able to talk about things
Rejected	Supported
	Helped

Method

Get two boxes and put a slit in each lid and label them:

Ways I want to be treated

Ways I don't want to be treated

Cut out the statements and ask the young woman to post the statements into the appropriate boxes.

Can you/she think of any other statements to add.

This can be used as a quick and simple exercise to focus on +/- aspects of relationships and what we want. When all the statements are posted the young woman can decide which box she would choose and which she would throw away (and could actually throw the box away in the session).

To extend the experience you could look at each box in turn and ask the young woman to pick out any of the things she has experienced. This could have the potential to become quite negative. The worker needs to be prepared for this and while acknowledging the young woman's experiences be ready to move on by:

- Moving on to look at what she would like from future relationships

- Moving on to how she achieves this i.e. how to work at relationships or a specific issue within relationships (Exercise such as: Friendship Goal/What Makes A Good Friend).

Developed by SJ and LR

Being ignored

Being left out

Being made fun of

Being put down

Being teased

Being hit

Being bullied

Being made to do things I don't like

Playing 'mind' games

Being nasty

Being hurtful

Treated badly

Made to feel stupid

Made to feel I don't belong

Rejected

Being listened to

Being included

Being appreciated

Being told nice things

Being treated kindly

Being respected

Being able to laugh together

Doing nice things

Treated fairly

Being given presents

Being loved

Being cared for

Being liked

Being able to talk about things

Supported

Helped

What Bugs Me?

Theme: Keeping relationships

Aim
To encourage the young woman to think about the problems she may face when forming and keeping relationships.

Materials
Ladybird picture, round stickers and colour pens.

Method
Encourage the young woman to think about what gets in the way for her when forming/keeping relationships, what bugs them about relationships. Using the stickers write down the issues and then place them on the ladybird spots. Discuss with the young woman how her fears, behaviour and anxieties can cause problems in relationships. What can she do to ensure that she feels safe and secure within the relationship? How does she know when the relationship is not meeting her needs?

Notes:
At the end of the session the young woman might like the ladybird to fly away!

Adapted by S.J. from ideas in MacFarlane and Cunningham (1991)

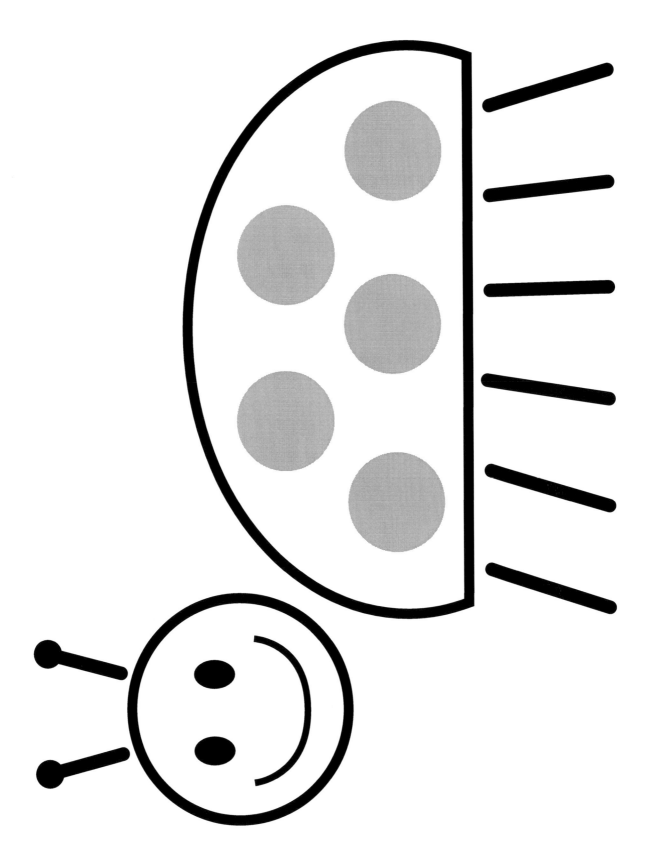

Taking Your Temperature – 2

Theme: Keeping Relationships

Aim
To help the young woman think about her responses to others.

Materials
Use the blank pro-forma from Session 3, plus some written scenarios of situations where conflict occurs and responses are out of context.

Method
Either one or both of you can think up some scenarios where conflict occurs. You may choose to use real or made up situations, it may be good to have a combination so that it does not become too personalised. If using real situations it may help to change names, locations etc., this again allows the young person to think more objectively and perhaps less defensively. She may choose to acknowledge the connection or not. What is important is that some space is created where she can think about her actions and explore different options if she wishes, or is ready to.

Decide where on the thermometer scale each situation goes, then compare responses. If they do not appear to 'fit', discuss why this is and what may be a response that would fit better.

Remember our responses become automatic over time, changes need to be thought about and take time to alter.

If the young woman identifies some ways she might alter her responses in some situations help her to identify a 'plan for change'. Create a reward system that encourages her, and, if she doesn't get it right first time, to try, and try again!

Adapted from MacFarlane and Cunningham

Theme: Keeping Relationships

Aim
To help the young woman have a framework for any changes she identifies, that provides small achievable steps.

Materials
Use the blank pro-forma, supported by the achievement certificate, or other reward system.

Method
This format can be used at any stage in the sessions where the young woman identifies an area for change. Support her in completing the pro-forma as realistically as possible. Remember, help her to keep the steps small and realistic so that positive outcomes are possible. Help to keep her motivated, and offer positive encouragement.

Developed by L.R. from MacFarlane and Cunningham and Anger Management Techniques

The thing I want to change is:

_____

_____

_____

_____

This is how I am going to bring about the change:

1 _____

2 _____

3 _____

4 _____

This is what I will do if it doesn't go right first time:
(what are the bits I did okay on and what bits did I not do)

1 _____

2 _____

3 _____

congratulations

You have worked hard on your plan for change!

Well Done

Keep going you are doing really well!

Signed _____

Date _____

....

(name)

congratulations

You have worked hard on your plan for change!

Well Done

Keep going you are doing really well!

Signed _____

Date _____

Session 7
Making Informed Choices

- What is okay/not okay?

- Making safe choices for ourselves and others

- Support networks and strategies to keep safe

looking glass framework

Session 7

Theme: Making Informed Choices

Aim
To provide a forum for looking at various scenarios around personal relationships and values.

Materials
Use the statement pro-formas, or include your own.

Method
This exercise can either be done using the sheets included in this pack as discussion points, or alternatively, transfer the statements onto pieces of card, place them face down between you and take it in turns choosing a card and sharing your views.

Making Informed Choices

What kinds of things do you look for in a boyfriend/girlfriend?

What is a good age to start going out with someone?

Who controls a person's sexual behaviour? The person themselves, or the person they are with? Can this be used as an excuse?

What kind of influence do things like drink or drugs have on our behaviours?

At what age do you think a girl can be a responsible parent?

At what age do you think a boy can be a responsible parent?

If you were 4 years old now, would you rather your parent was 17, 21 or 25? Why?

Do you think you may want to have children? If yes, what age do you think you would be ready to be a parent?

Do you think the parents of a child should get married? Does this make a difference to anyone?

Is being a virgin cool?

What does 'abstinence' mean and is it okay in today's society?

What is it okay to tell your friends about your relationship?

What do you say if a good friend asks you personal questions that you don't really want to answer?

Which person/people do you go to for good advice?

How do you know that it is good advice?

How do you tell someone that you have 'finished' with them?

How would you want to be told if someone had 'finished' with you?

From T Cavanagh-Johnson (1998)

Snakes and Ladders Game

Theme: Making Informed Choices

Aim
To give the young woman the opportunity to explore various scenarios around making safe choices.

Materials
Snakes and ladders board game and choices cards (make own).

Method
Play the snakes and ladders game as normal, but when the person lands on a ladder or a snake they have to take a choices card. If they answer the question safely the person moves up the ladder and if it is unsafe they move down the snake.

Choices Cards – examples

1. If a good-looking young man in a flashy car stops by you and asks you to come over do you?
    a) Go over and have a chat.
    b) Get in the car with him.
    c) Ignore him.

2. You are with a group of friends and are desperate for a cigarette, but have no money. One of the lads says he will let you have one of his if you will go round the back with him, do you?
    a) Tell him you are not that kind of girl, but go anyway.
    b) Tell him to get lost.
    c) Go round the back and see what happens.

3. You have met this lad that you really fancy, but you do not know him very well. He has asked you to meet him, do you?
    a) Get dressed up and go and meet him on your own.
    b) Tell him you need to get to know him better first.
    c) Take a friend with you.

4. Your boyfriend is putting pressure on you to have sex with him, do you?

    a)   Tell him he will have to wait until you are ready.

    b)   Have sex with him, because if you don't you will lose him.

    c)   Let him do a bit of heavy petting to keep him quiet.

5. You are having trouble with a couple of girls at school, they will not leave you alone, do you?

    a)   Challenge them to fight and hope they will say 'no'.

    b)   Hide in your bedroom and don't go to school.

    c)   Tell an adult that you trust that you are being bullied.

Note:

Make the choices cards, reflecting the young woman's individual needs.

Developed by S.J. Pro-forma available in Draw on Your Emotions

Session 8
Ending the Set of Sessions

- Reviewing work undertaken

- Planning further sessions, if appropriate

- Ending on a positive note, positive affirmations to the young person

looking glass framework

Theme: Endings

Ending the piece of work should allow for:

- A recognition of what you have learnt about the young woman's personality, view of life, her experiences, strengths, and needs.
- An understanding of what future key-working sessions will be like.
- Moving onto more focused areas of work, if appropriate.
- Having some fun together in recognition of the work undertaken, and experiences shared.

You could use some of the exercises from Session 4, if not already used:

- Flower Petals
- CD Box
- Life Ladder

Or you could have a fun session using clay, play-dough or cornflour, and just enjoy making shapes and feeling the textures – it's fun and very therapeutic!

An alternative way of ending is to use the Box of Treasures exercise.

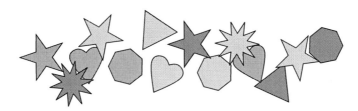

Box of Treasures

Theme: Endings

Aim

To end the sessions in a positive way reflecting on what you have learnt about the young woman's strengths, resilience and positive characteristics.

Materials

A box and materials to decorate it, some gem stones, or ready cut out shapes (stars, circles, diamonds, flowers), glitter, sequins and felt tip pens to decorate.

Method

The young woman decorates the box. Each of you then take a shape representing each of the sessions. Each of you think about the session and write your thoughts about:

- what she learnt from the session

- strengths/positives that were identified

Each of you then talk about this, before she decorates it and adds it to her box of 'treasures' to keep.

An alternative method is to have a different coloured gem-stone for each session. Each time she chooses a stone to represent a session repeat the process of identifying strengths/positives and what she contributed to the session, or learnt from it, before she adds it to her box.

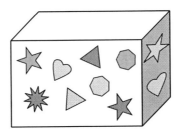

Developed by SJ/CP/LR

**Think
POSITIVE**

**When someone likes you
YOU BEGIN TO LIKE YOURSELF**

**When someone respects you
YOU BEGIN TO RESPECT YOURSELF**

**When someone sees the strength in you
YOU FEEL STRONG**

**When someone believes in you
YOU START TO BELIEVE IN YOURSELF**

**BEWARE!!
positive thoughts are catching**

Resources

The exercises in this pack come from a range of sources. Some of the exercises were developed with the young women specifically during this piece of work, some have been adapted from other ideas, and some have been used over many years and the original source cannot be remembered!

Books

Bremner, J. and Hillin, A. (1994) *Sexuality, Young People and Care*. Lyme Regis, Russell House Publishing.

Carroll, J. (1988) *Introduction to Therapeutic Play*. Oxford, Blackwell Science Ltd.

Cavanagh Johnson, T. (1998) *Sexuality Curriculum for Abused Children and Young Adolescents and Their Parents*. California, self-published.

Cavanagh Johnson, T. (1998) *Treatment Exercises for Child Abuse Victims and Children with Sexual Behaviour Problems*. California, self-published.

Cunningham, C. and MacFarlane, K. (1991) *When Children Molest Children: Strategies*. Orwell, VT, Safer Society Press.

Fitzpatrick, P., Clarke, K. and Higgins, P. (1994) *The Chalkface Project: Self-esteem*. Milton Keynes The Chalkface Project.

Ironside, V. (1994) *The Huge Bag of Worries*. Edinburgh, Children 1st.

James, B. (1989) *Treating Traumatised Children*. Lexington, MA, Lexington Books.

Kelly, A. (1996) *Talkabout: A Social Communication Skills Package*. Oxon, Speechmark Publishing.

King, P. (1989) *Talking Pictures*. London, BAAF.

MacFarlane, K. and Cunningham, C. (1988) *Steps to Healthy Touching*. Kidrights.

Nightingale, C. (1987) *The Chalkface Project:Exercises to Improve Self-knowledge and Self-esteem*. Milton Keynes, The Chalkface Project.

Oaklander, V. (1988) *Windows to our Children*. N.Y., Gestalt Journal Press.

PACE *A Handbook for Parents of Children with Attachment Disorder*. PACE.

Redgrave, K. (1987) *Child's Play*. Cheadle, Boys' & Girls' Welfare Society.

Striker, T. S. and Kimmel, E. (1978) *The Anti-colouring Book*. London, Scholastic Publications Ltd.

Sunderland, M. and Engelheart, P. (1993) *Draw on Your Emotions*. Oxon., Winslow Press.

Szirom, T. and Dyson, S. (1954) *Greater Expectations*. Fitzroy, YWCA of Australia.

Trower, T. (1995) *The Self Control Patrol Workbook*. N.Y., Plainview, Childswork Childsplay.

Williams, E. and Barlow, R. (1998) *Anger Control Training*. Oxon., Winslow Press.

Games

All About Me – Barnado's

Proud to be Me

The Grapevine Game – Sex Education Game

The Mad Sad Glad Game

The Helping, Sharing and Caring Game

The above games have been used by the team and are felt to have been useful tools to aid communication.

A wide range of games are available through the 'Being Yourself' Catalogue, Smallwood Publishing – tel: 01304 226900 fax: 01304 226700.